D0772837

Why Are You So Sad?

A CHILD'S
BOOK ABOUT
PARENTAL
DEPRESSION

To my husband Leonard, my daughter Rebecca,
and to all the clients/patients over the years
who have inspired this book — BA

For my mother — NW

Copyright © 2002 by Magination Press. All rights reserved.
Except as permitted under the United States Copyright Act of 1976,
no part of this publication may be reproduced or distributed in any form
or by any means, or stored in a database or retrieval system,
without the prior written permission of the publisher.

Published by
MAGINATION PRESS
An Educational Publishing Foundation Book
American Psychological Association
750 First Street, NE
Washington, DC 20002

For more information about our books, including a complete catalog,
please write to us, call 1-800-374-2721, or visit our website at
www.maginationpress.com.

Editor: Darcie Conner Johnston
Art Director: Susan K. White
The text type is Stone Informal
Printed by Phoenix Color, Rockaway, New Jersey

Library of Congress Cataloging-in-Publication Data
Andrews, Beth.
Why are you so sad? : a child's book about parental depression /
written by Beth Andrews ; illustrated by Nicole Wong.
p. cm.
Summary: For children with a depressed parent, this interactive book defines
depression, identifies depression treatment, and provides many self-help options
for those coping with a depressed parent. Includes a note to parents.
ISBN 1-55798-8366 hc : alk. paper — ISBN 1-55798-8870 sc : alk. paper
1. Depression, Mental—Juvenile literature.
2. Parents—Mental health—Juvenile literature.
3. Children of depressed persons—Juvenile literature.
[1. Depression, Mental.] I. Wong, Nicole E., ill. II. Title.

RC537.A566 2002
616.85'27—dc21   2002004299

Manufactured in the United States of America
10 9 8 7 6 5 4 3 2 1

Why Are You So Sad?

A CHILD'S BOOK ABOUT PARENTAL DEPRESSION

written by Beth Andrews, L.C.S.W.
illustrated by Nicole Wong

MAGINATION PRESS • WASHINGTON, DC

This book is just for you. It's all about a special kind of problem called *depression* that moms and dads can get.

Depression is a problem with feelings. You can think of depression as feelings that aren't the way they are supposed to be, or as feelings that have gotten sick. Moms and dads feel bad when they are depressed.

Parents don't feel bad on purpose. They don't want to feel bad, just like you don't want to feel bad when you are sick with a cold or the flu and have to stay in bed when you would rather be outside playing. It just happens sometimes.

You can't catch depression like you can catch a cold. And it's harder to see than a cold. When you have a cold, you might sneeze and cough and have a stuffy nose. But when grown-ups are depressed, they usually look pretty much the same as always, even though they feel bad inside.

Can you draw a picture of your parent who is depressed?

Sometimes parents act different when they're depressed. They may not be able to sleep. Or they might sleep all the time and have a hard time getting out of bed, even to make your dinner or to play with you.

They might not eat and get thinner. Or they might eat too much and get bigger. Or they might look just the same.

They might forget things that are important, like where the keys are or that they promised to take you to the park.

They might not have the energy to play with you like they used to.

They might get mad or
cranky and yell a lot.

They might cry and cry,
and act very sad.

Sometimes parents might even
smile and act happy, when they
really feel very sad inside.

How does your depressed parent act? Draw a picture.

Here is some good news.
There are lots of things that
depressed moms and dads can
do to help themselves feel
better. For one thing, they can
talk to a *therapist* or *counselor*.
That's a person who has gone
to a special school to learn
how to help your parent solve
problems and feel better.

Sometimes they go to a doctor who gives them medicine that can help them feel better.

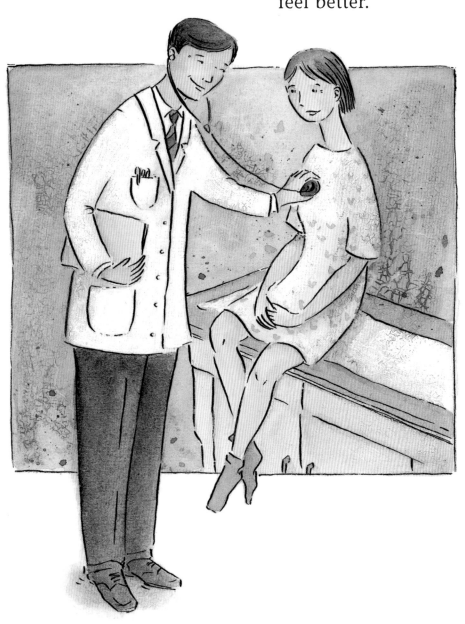

If the depression gets bad enough,
they might have to go to the hospital
for a few days. There they will get medicine,
rest, and spend a lot of time talking about
their problems. This will help them feel better,
so that they can come home and feel good
like they did before they got depressed.

Here are some important questions to ask if your parent has to go to the hospital.

Who will take care of me while you are at the hospital? *(There will always be a grown-up to take care of you, of course. You just want to know who it will be.)*

Will I sleep in my bed or at someone else's house? *(Sometimes kids stay with a close friend's family or a relative.)*

Can I call you and come to visit you?

Do you know when you will be coming home?

Do you have any other questions that you want to ask your parent?

Kids have lots of feelings when their mom or dad gets depressed.

Do you ever feel like this?

angry

scared

guilty

lonely

embarrassed

sad

worried

hurt

bored

Kids sometimes worry about having these feelings,
but they are very common feelings to have when a parent
is depressed. Whatever you feel is okay.

Draw a picture about what you are feeling today.

Sometimes kids are mixed up or have a lot of different
feelings at once. We call that feeling *confused*.
It's very common to feel confused, and that's okay, too.

Sometimes kids worry that the depression is their fault. It's important to remember that it is not your fault. You didn't cause it by being bad, or by not being nice or helpful, or by *anything* you did.

Sometimes kids think that they can do something to fix the depression. But you can't fix it for your parent by being really good or helpful, or by joking around, or by being naughty, or by anything else you do. Just like you didn't do anything to cause the depression, you can't do anything to fix it. Therapists and doctors can help your mom or dad fix their depression, but that's not your job.

What have you tried to do, thinking that you could make it better? Draw a picture.

It's important to remember that your mom or dad still loves you. Depressed parents might have a hard time showing you sometimes, because they feel so bad. But they do love you.

And you still love them. Even if you feel angry at them. Did you know that you can love someone and be angry at them at the same time? When you feel angry, it can be hard to remember that the loving feelings will come back. But they always do.

It also helps to remember that you are not alone. Lots of kids have these feelings when their mom or dad is depressed. And there are lots of adults who care about you and your feelings. Even your depressed mom or dad cares. Other caring adults may include other family members, grandparents, aunts and uncles, teachers, neighbors, babysitters, and parents of friends.

There are many things that kids can do to help themselves feel better and live more easily with moms or dads who are depressed. For one thing, you can tell them how you feel. And you can ask for what you need. If your mom or dad can't give you what you need right now, you can ask another caring adult you know and trust for help.

You can also talk with these grown-ups about your feelings. Talking about feelings can help us feel better. Who are your favorite people to talk to?

Draw a picture of them here.

It helps a lot to spend time playing and talking with your friends, and doing all the things that are fun for you. It's okay to enjoy yourself, even when your mom or dad is feeling bad.

You can draw pictures about your mom or dad,
or the depression, or your feelings. Drawing pictures
can really help with feelings that bother kids.

What would you like to draw here?

If you are feeling angry,

you can punch something soft,

like a pillow,

or you can go outside

and kick a ball or

just jump up and down

to get some of the mad

feelings out.

Sometimes kids even visit
a therapist. When kids go to
a therapist, they talk, play,
and draw pictures about the
things that bother them when
their mom or dad is
depressed. Therapists know
how to help kids feel better
with all the different feelings
they might have.

Having a mom or dad with depression can be hard, no doubt about it. But you can make things easier for yourself while your parent is getting better. Just remember:

1 Depression is a problem with feelings.

2 It's not your fault.

3 You can't fix it.

4 It's okay to have whatever feelings you have about it.

5 Your parent still loves you, and you still love your parent.

6 There are lots and lots of things that you can do to help yourself feel better.

Note to Parents and Other Caregivers

BY BETH ANDREWS, L.C.S.W.
AND JANE ANNUNZIATA, PSY.D.

Clinical depression is a painful and confusing experience that affects at least 15 percent of American adults each year. Children are highly tuned in to their parents: what affects the parent affects the child, so when a parent is depressed the child also experiences pain and confusion. Children may feel scared, lonely, worried, angry, or sad themselves. However, unlike adults, they often don't have the skills to understand or express their feelings. They may also have difficulty expressing these feelings when a parent is already struggling, fearing that they'll further burden their mom or dad.

HOW THIS BOOK CAN HELP

The purpose of this book is to help children:

- understand what depression is and what it is not;
- identify and understand their own feelings and reactions;
- cope with their own feelings and with their parent's depression;
- know that they are not alone and that help is available.

This book is designed to be read by or to children with the help of a parent (or therapist, counselor, teacher, or other caring adult) and to be used as a catalyst for further discussion. It is not meant to be completed in only one sitting. Instead, start at the beginning and read one section or topic at a time, returning to any section as often as your child likes or needs to.

This book encourages children to draw their feelings and experiences, because making pictures is a good way for them to express themselves, and it seems to provide a release from the stress of uncomfortable feelings. This is especially true because children often don't know the words to use to describe what they think or feel. Let the child draw in this book where prompted, and have more paper available for any additional pictures that he or she might wish to create. Talk about the drawings and your child's feelings and thoughts as much as your child might want. If your child is reluctant, it's helpful for you to say what he or she would probably be saying if not for the fear of hurting your feelings.

HELPING YOUR CHILD COPE WITH PARENTAL DEPRESSION

Sitting down with your child and this book is an excellent way to begin. It will answer many questions that your child has, suggest a number of ways to cope, open up communication between parent and child, and give you ideas on how to talk with your child about your depression. Here are some on-going ways you can help your child cope with your depression:

Listen to your child. Help him or her identify and name feelings, and make sure your child knows that it's okay to talk about any feeling with you. Respond in a nonjudgmental way, and communicate your acceptance of whatever feelings emerge—especially the more negative ones, such as anger, worry, and so on. As stated above, kids are often reluctant to admit to negative feelings and may deny having them. When this happens, try responding with gentle humor. For example, if you say, "I'll bet you were pretty annoyed when I was too tired to drive you to your soccer game," and your child shrugs and says, "That's okay," you could respond with, "Well, you must be the only kid in the world who wouldn't get angry! I know I would have been hopping mad!"

Negative feelings are normal. Let your child know that the feelings he or she has about your depression are quite common and to be expected. Specifically, when you are reading page 16, which lists a number of common feelings, talk about why children feel these ways, in order to give your child more permission for these difficult feelings. For example:

- Children might feel *angry* because their parent is too preoccupied to focus on them.
- They might feel *scared* because they're worried something bad will happen to mom or dad.
- They might feel *guilty* because they feel angry at their parent.
- They might feel *lonely* because their parent is so self-focused.
- They might feel *embarrassed* because their parent acts in ways that make them uncomfortable.
- They might feel *sad* because they are absorbing some of their parent's sad feelings.
- They might feel *worried* because they wonder if the parent won't get better.
- They might feel *hurt* because their parent snaps at them and is impatient because of the depression.
- They might feel *bored* because their parent is too depressed to play with them or to take them places.

Affirm your love. Reassure your child that you love him or her, even though your actions when you are irritable, preoccupied, or withdrawn might not seem very loving.

It's not their fault. Reinforce the fact that your depression is not their fault. Children often have what is known as "magical thinking" and may think they did some-

thing to cause it, or that they can fix it. Emphasize that it is not their job to fix your depression, and that it is *your* job, with the help of your therapists, medication, and other supports you may have.

Plan and be positive. Let your child know your plan for resolving your problems, and offer optimism that your depression is treatable and that you will feel better. For example, you can read this book together, and let your child know what steps you are taking as you read about them in the book. For example, "I am seeing a therapist, whose name is Dr. Lee, every week." You could also mention other, concrete parts of a plan that your therapist or doctor might recommend, such as physical exercise.

Practice honesty with restraint. Don't leave your child wondering what is going on. When children have to fill in the blanks themselves, they may imagine the worst. Telling the truth produces trust and a sense of security. However, it is important that you avoid telling them more than they need to know.

- Use restraint when expressing your emotions, and use good judgment when disclosing information. A good guideline is to tell them what they need to know for things to make sense or to calm their unwarranted fears. Children should not be told about such things as the depth of a parent's depression, suicidal thoughts, or other self-harming behaviors or ideas.
- Don't use euphemisms or tell outright lies. For example, it's best to tell your child, "I am going to the hospital, where my doctors and therapists will help me get better so that I can come back home and be my old self again." Don't say that you are "going away for a little while." A child may wonder why he or she can't come too, or whether you're really coming back. The truth, disclosed appropriately, is generally

most reassuring for the child.

- Do not expect or allow your child to be your shoulder to cry on. If you are depressed, you need other adults, including professional help, to talk to about your problems and feelings.

Ask for help to get your kids' needs met.
Try to pay attention to and help your children identify their needs. If you are too depressed to meet all of these needs, find other trusted adults who can. It's okay to ask for help, and it's very beneficial for children when their emotional and practical needs continue to be adequately met in spite of the parent's depression. Do not rely on your child to care for younger siblings, or to meet your needs.

The role of the non-depressed parent.
In two-parent homes, the parent who is not depressed has a crucial role in making sure that children's needs continue to be met. This parent can also help children weather the depression and make sense of it by setting a tone of open communication, encouraging them to ask questions and express their feelings and thoughts. He or she can help the depressed parent give appropriate information and reassurance to the children. And finally, one of the most important charges of the non-depressed parent is to make sure that the child's life stays as normal as possible: routines, rules, schedules, chores, friends, playtime, school, activities, and discipline should all be maintained as usual.

Get professional help. If you are not sure where to go, ask for a referral from your family doctor, a counselor at your child's school, your clergyperson, state or local mental health associations, or a friend or neighbor who has had a good treatment experience. Or you can look up "Mental Health Centers" in your phone book. If you have thought about suicide, please get help now. Depression is very treatable with counseling and medications. You, the parent, are the most important person in your child's life. Your child needs you!

RISK FOR DEPRESSION IN THE CHILD

Parental depression can put a child at risk for childhood depression, depression later in life, and other mental health problems. However, as we just mentioned, depression is very treatable, for both children and adults. The earlier you intervene, the easier it is to treat. If you are concerned that your child may be feeling depressed or overly anxious, talk about it with him or her and get help for your child. It's always better to get your concerns checked out and ruled out than to worry and wonder.

There are several things that parents can do to help minimize the risk that their children will develop depression either as a child or later in life:

- Seek help for the depressed parent as early as possible, before serious depressive symptoms set in.
- Seek help for children as early as possible to rule out depression or other behavioral, psychological, or mental health problems.
- Encourage constructive and consistent expression of children's feelings, so that they don't keep feelings bottled inside or deal with them inappropriately (e.g., exploding, being mean to siblings, etc.).
- Encourage constructive techniques for coping with feelings for both children and parents, such as talking about feelings, physical exercise, drawing feelings, journaling, and playing out feelings with toys.
- Notify the child's doctor about the family history of depression so that he or she can keep an eye on the situation.
- Encourage children to develop meaningful peer relationships, hobbies, activities, and interests at all stages of development.

— *B.A. and J.A.*

32